HERE WE GO ROUND
THE
MULBERRY BUSH

ILLUSTRATED BY JENNY RENDALL

Houghton Mifflin Company • Boston
Atlanta • Dallas • Geneva, Illinois • Palo Alto • Princeton

Here we go round the mulberry bush,

The mulberry bush, the mulberry bush.

Here we go round the mulberry bush,

On a cold and frosty morning.

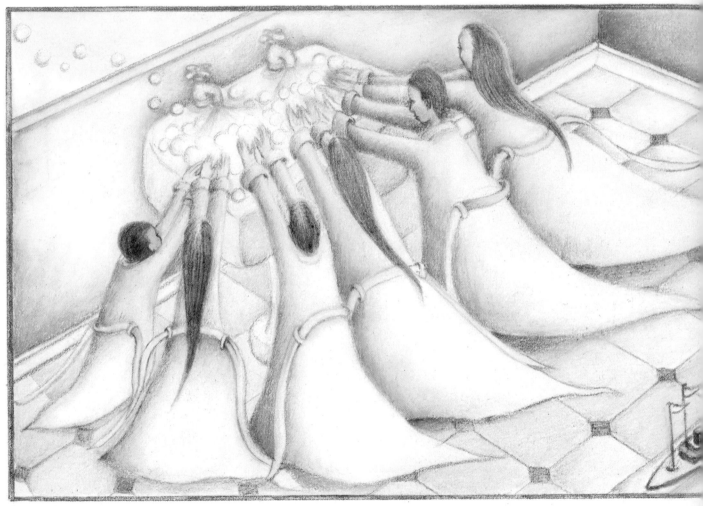

4

This is the way we wash our hands,

Wash our hands, wash our hands.

This is the way we wash our hands,

On a cold and frosty morning.

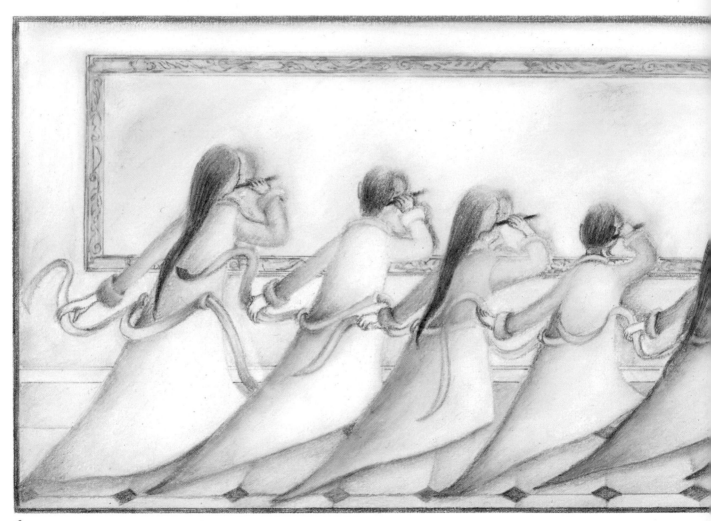

6

This is the way we brush our teeth,

Brush our teeth, brush our teeth.

This is the way we brush our teeth,

On a cold and frosty morning.

This is the way we comb our hair,

Comb our hair, comb our hair.

This is the way we comb our hair,

On a cold and frosty morning.

This is the way we wave good-bye,

Wave good-bye, wave good-bye.

This is the way we wave good-bye,

On a cold and frosty morning.

This is the way we go to school,

Go to school, go to school.

This is the way we go to school,

On a cold and frosty morning.

14

Here we go round the mulberry bush,
The mulberry bush, the mulberry bush.
Here we go round the mulberry bush,
On a cold and frosty morning.

Here We Go Round the Mulberry Bush

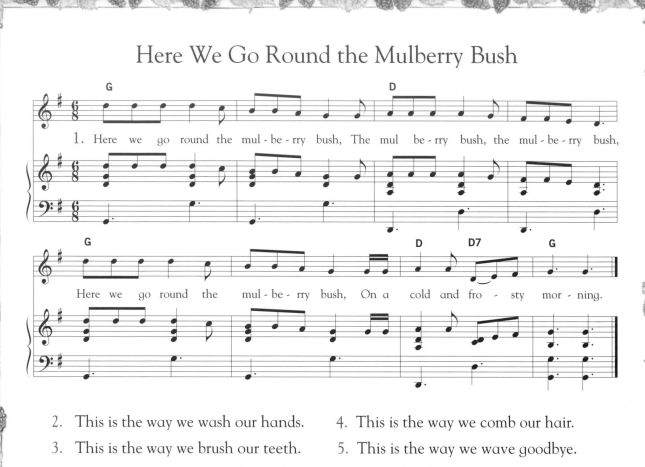

1. Here we go round the mul-be-rry bush, The mul-be-rry bush, the mul-be-rry bush,

Here we go round the mul-be-rry bush, On a cold and fro-sty mor-ning.

2. This is the way we wash our hands.

3. This is the way we brush our teeth.

4. This is the way we comb our hair.

5. This is the way we wave goodbye.

6. This is the way we go to school.